INSTANT POT
FAST AND EASY

Recipes for Cooking with Little Effort Less Time

EDDIE RONNY

Table of Contents

Sommario

INTRODUCTION 7

WHAT IS AN INSTANT POT AND HOW DO YOU USE IT? 7
WHAT IS AN INSTANT POT? 7
BUT WHAT DOES THIS THING DO THAT'S SPECIAL? 8
WHAT THE INSTANT POT LOOKS LIKE 8
HOW MUCH WHAT THE INSTANT POT? 9
BUT WHAT DO I COOK IN THIS INSTANT POT? 9

CHICKEN 11

MOM'S ORANGE CHICKEN 12
FAVORITE BBQ MEATLOAF 14
THAI RED DUCK 16
EXOTIC DUCK MASALA 17

PORK 18

GARDEN VEGETABLE SOUP WITH PORK 19
BARBECUED PORK SPARE RIBS 20
COUNTRY-STYLE PORK MEATBALLS 22
SPICY SAUSAGE BAKE 24

BEEF 26

GROUND BEEF SIRLOIN SOUP 27
STICKY BEEF WITH BROWN SAUCE 28
HEARTY GROUND BEEF FRITTATA 30
GRANNY'S CLASSIC BEEF AND GRAVY 31

SOUPS 32

RED LENTIL AND SPINACH SOUP 33
GRANDMA'S NOODLE SOUP 35
AUTHENTIC FRENCH ONION SOUP 36
CREAMED CORN AND CHICKEN SOUP 38

STEWS 39

NORTHERN ITALIAN BEEF STEW 40
ITALIAN BEEF RAGÙ 42
RICH AND EASY CHICKEN PURLOO 44
SEAFOOD AND VEGETABLE RAGOUT 45

STOCKS AND SAUCES 47

CLASSIC FISH STOCK 48
ROASTED VEGETABLE STOCK 49
SPANISH CHORIZO SAUCE 51
SIMPLE COURT BOUILLON 52

FISH AND SEAFOOD 54

TILAPIA FILLETS WITH CREMINI MUSHROOMS 55

SAUCY PARMESAN COD WITH BASMATI RICE 57
SAUSAGE AND PRAWN BOIL WITH OLD BAY SAUCE 58
SPICY THAI PRAWNS 60

BEANS – PASTA - GRAINS..**61**

BULGUR WHEAT WITH PICO DE GALLO 62
OATMEAL WITH BANANAS AND WALNUTS..63
GRANDMOTHER'S BUTTERMILK CORNBREAD 65
MILLET PORRIDGE WITH ALMONDS AND RAISINS 66

LOW CARB..**68**

BACON FRITTATA MUFFINS 69
GREEK-STYLE MUSHROOM MUFFINS..70
ZUCCHINI CARDAMOM BREAD 72
CAULIFLOWER BREAKFAST CUPS 73

VEGAN **75**

TRADITIONAL RUSSIAN BORSCHT..76
PURPLE CABBAGE WITH BASMATI RICE 78
QUINOA AND CHICKPEA BOWL..79
GREAT NORTHERN BEANS ON TOAST 81

VEGETABLE AND SIDE DISHES..**82**

VEGAN BAKED BEANS 83
PUNJABI BEAN CURRY 85
PARMESAN BRUSSELS SPROUTS 86
AROMATIC SNOW PEAS 88

RICE...**89**

MEXICAN-STYLE SALSA RICE..90
PULAO RICE PAKISTANI STYLE 91
CHICKEN, BROCCOLI AND RICE CASSEROLE 93
PERFECT SUSHI RICE..94

SNACKS AND APPETIZERS **95**

RANCH-STYLE POPCORN 96
CHINESE STICKY BABY CARROTS 97
CRISPY CHICKEN DRUMETTES 99
PARTY DEVILED EGGS..100

DESSERTS..**102**

CHERRY AND ALMOND CRISP PIE 103
COUNTRY-STYLE APPLES..104
CRANBERRY-MAPLE RICE PUDDING 106
PERFECT HOLIDAY CUPCAKES..107

Introduction

What is an Instant Pot and how do you use it?

Some people have fallen in love with their Instant Pots. They might love blenders, adore their flaming slow cookers, and need a robot in the kitchen, but the Instant Pot is the one they can't live without anymore.

What is an Instant Pot?

It's a small appliance with huge potential, and in the size of a large pot, it packs an electronic pressure cooker, slow cooker, rice cooker, and yogurt maker. Ingenious isn't it?

If you are already the proud owner of a traditional pressure cooker that is now keeping company with a dust colony in the back of the last kitchen cabinet because of the fear you have that it will explode in your hand, I feel like reassuring you immediately. What makes this new generation of digital pressure cookers different are just the safety features, including sensors that keep track of temperature and pressure level.

All you have to do is connect it to electricity and push a button, the instant pot will do it all by itself. It's as simple to use as the slow cooker, only the cooking times are significantly less.

But what does this thing do that's special?

For one, it cooks whole pieces of meat divinely and super fast. After just under 90 minutes, an entire pork shoulder is so tender that it can be cut with a breadstick, and it tastes amazing, too. The same recipe made with a slow cooker takes about 7 hours to achieve the same result and still the meat isn't as juicy and flavorful. The key to being happy with your electric pressure cooker is to choose recipes where you need to get a smooth and juicy result.

What the Instant Pot looks like

It is a large stainless steel pressure cooker with different capacities (and different prices depending on which one you choose), it has a lid and lots of buttons that will help you set the program you prefer, decide the temperature and the time you want it to start cooking. This is in case you want it to prepare dinner when you are not there and find it ready as soon as you cross the threshold of the house. It is easy to wash because inside the appliance there is a removable stainless steel pot, which you can remove and wash and even use on the stove if you miss one. Inside the package, you will also find a steel basket if you want to try steaming. And the instruction booklet. I know we live in an age where it is no longer used to stop and read how to use something, we are all learned, but do it because this thing is very easy to use but not as intuitive. It only takes 5 minutes for the basic functions. Invest this time for the sake of your future dinners. Don't be fooled by the name, because Instant is just that, the name. It's a quick way to prepare recipes that would otherwise take a lot of time and energy to make. But you must calculate the downtime well. Once the pot is closed it must come under pressure, and it will take at least 15 minutes, when it has finished cooking your food it must slowly release the steam safely before opening, and even for this operation count about ten minutes. However, I feel like I can tell you from the results you get, that the game is worth the candle.

How much what the Instant Pot?

The cost depends a lot on which model you want to buy. The basic model has all the features you need to start cooking with an electric pressure stove, the only thing you can't prepare with the basic model is yogurt which is available from the slightly higher model, the Duo. The Duo Plus is the best-selling model of all since it can also prepare cakes, cook eggs and even sterilize food, and it costs twice as much as the basic model. Then some ultra-technological models have buttons to customize the cooking endlessly, Bluetooth, apps, programming complex recipes, and so on. I'm still of the opinion that to start with, the basic model will bring you joy.

But what do I cook in this Instant Pot?

In this pot of wonders, you can cook all the meat you can think of. Especially large cuts, which would take a long time to cook the traditional way. For example, you could try cooking veal with tuna sauce, even trying the low-temperature function. In addition to the old-fashioned way, you could also try your hand at more daring preparations such as veal ravioli with tuna sauce. You will also obtain fantastic results with braised meats, and I recommend trying braised veal in Barolo wine. But if you're not in the mood for meat, you can always use your digital pressure cooker to cook lentils and turn them into a delicious soup as well. You can prepare whole chicken in it, but be sure to remember to use the sauté function. It will be your special tool for cooking meatloaf. You can also prepare potatoes, especially if they are meant to be mashed.

In this book, you have several very appetizing recipes to use with your Instant Pot. Once you gain skill and experience in using this fantastic appliance, you won't be able to do without it. Enjoy!

EDDIE RONNY

Chicken

Mom's Orange Chicken

(Ready in about 15 minutes | Servings 4)

Per serving: 337 Calories; 26g Fat; 8.8g Carbs; 18.9g Protein; 2g Sugars

Ingredients

1 tablespoon olive oil
2/3 pound ground chicken
1/3 pound bacon, chopped
2 tablespoons sherry wine
1 medium red onion, chopped
2 garlic cloves, minced
1 jalapeno pepper, chopped
Sea salt and ground black pepper, to taste
1 teaspoon paprika
Fresh juice and zest of 1/2 orange
1 tablespoon arrowroot powder

Directions

Press the "Sauté" button and heat the oil until sizzling. Sear the chicken and bacon until they areslightly brown.

Add the sherry wine and stir with a wooden spoon, scraping up the browned bits on the bottomof the pan. Add the red onion, garlic, and jalapeno pepper; stir to combine.

Season with salt, black pepper, and paprika. Pour in 1 cup of water. Secure the lid. Choose "Poultry" mode. Cook for 5 minutes at High pressure. Once cooking iscomplete, use a quick pressure release; carefully remove the lid.

Add the orange juice and zest; stir in the arrowroot powder. Press the "Sauté" button andsimmer, stirring occasionally, until it thickens. Bon appétit!

Favorite BBQ Meatloaf

(Ready in about 45 minutes | Servings 5)

Per serving: 450 Calories; 27.8g Fat; 15.6g Carbs; 34.2g Protein; 5.9g Sugars

Ingredients

1 tablespoons olive oil
1 tablespoon Worcestershire sauce
1 pound ground chicken
1/2 pound ground beef
1/2 cup crackers, crushed
1/4 cup Parmesan cheese, grated
1 medium carrot, grated
2 sweet peppers, deseeded and chopped
1 chili pepper, deseeded and finely chopped
1 onion, finely chopped
2 garlic cloves, minced
1 egg, beaten
1/2 cup BBQ sauce
Smoked salt flakes and freshly ground black pepper, to taste

Directions

Place a steamer rack inside the inner pot; add 1/2 cup water. Cut 1 sheet of heavy-duty foil andbrush with cooking spray. In large mixing dish, thoroughly combine all ingredients until mixed well. Shape the meat mixture into a loaf; place the meatloaf in the center of the foil. Wrap yourmeatloaf in the foil and lower onto the steamer rack.

Secure the lid. Choose the "Poultry" mode and cook for 30 minutes at High pressure. Oncecooking is complete, use a quick pressure release; carefully remove the lid.

Then, transfer your meatloaf to a cutting board. Let it stand for 10 minutes before cutting andserving. To serve, brush with some extra BBQ sauce, if desired. Bon appétit!

Thai Red Duck

(Ready in about 50 minutes | Servings 4)

Per serving: 467 Calories; 27.8g Fat; 6.8g Carbs; 47.6g Protein; 2.5g Sugars

Ingredients
1 tablespoon Thai red curry paste
Zest and juice of 1 fresh lime
pounds duck breast1 tablespoon olive oil
1 1/2 teaspoon black peppercorns, crushed
1 teaspoon cayenne pepper
1 teaspoon sea salt
4 garlic cloves, minced
2 2 thyme sprigs, chopped
rosemary sprigs, chopped
1 cup light coconut milk
1/2 cup chicken broth, preferably homemade
1/4 small pack coriander, roughly chopped

Directions
Combine the red curry paste with the lime zest and juice; rub the mixture all over the duck breastand leave it to marinate for 30 minutes. Press the "Sauté" button and heat the oil until sizzling. Cook the duck breast until slightly brownon both sides.

Then, season the duck breasts with the peppercorns, cayenne pepper, and salt. Add the garlic,thyme, rosemary, coconut milk, and chicken broth.

Secure the lid. Choose the "Poultry" mode and cook for 15 minutes at High pressure. Oncecooking is complete, use a quick pressure release; carefully remove the lid.

Garnish with chopped coriander and serve warm. Bon appétit!

Exotic Duck Masala

(Ready in about 35 minutes | Servings 6)

Per serving: 539 Calories; 38.2g Fat; 5.2g Carbs; 45.1g Protein; 2.7g Sugars

Ingredients

2 tablespoons butter, melted at room temperature
3 pounds duck thighs
Sea salt, to taste
1/4 teaspoon crushed black peppercorns, or more to taste
1 teaspoon ginger powder
1/2 teaspoon chili powder
1 tablespoon rosemary
1 tablespoon sage
1/2 teaspoon allspice berries, lightly crushed
2 garlic cloves, sliced
1/2 cup tomato paste
1/2 cup bone broth
1 tablespoon Garam masala
1 small bunch of fresh coriander, roughly chopped

Directions

Press the "Sauté" button and melt the butter. Now, cook the duck thighs until golden brown onboth sides. Add all seasonings.
Next, stir in the garlic, tomato paste, broth, and Garam masala.
Secure the lid. Choose the "Manual" mode and cook for 25 minutes at High pressure. Oncecooking is complete, use a quick pressure release; carefully remove the lid.
Serve with fresh coriander. Enjoy!

Pork

Garden Vegetable Soup with Pork

(Ready in about 40 minutes | Servings 4)

Per serving: 264 Calories; 8.6g Fat; 6.6g Carbs; 38.2g Protein; 2.5g
Sugars

Ingredients
1 tablespoon olive oil
1 pound pork stew meat, cubed
4 cups beef bone broth
1 cup scallion, chopped
1 carrot, sliced
1 celery, sliced
1 turnip, peeled and sliced
Sea salt and ground black pepper, to taste
2 cups spinach

Directions
Press the "Sauté" button to preheat your Instant Pot; heat the oil. Now,
sear the meat until it isdelicately browned.
Add the remaining ingredients, except for the spinach.
Secure the lid. Choose the "Soup" setting and cook at High pressure
for 30 minutes. Oncecooking is complete, use a quick pressure release;
carefully remove the lid.
Add the spinach to the Instant Pot; seal the lid and allow it to sit in the
residual heat until wilted.Ladle the soup into individual bowls and serve
right away. Bon appétit!

Barbecued Pork Spare Ribs

(Ready in about 45 minutes | Servings 4)

Per serving: 500 Calories; 28.6g Fat; 8.9g Carbs; 49.2g Protein; 6.1g Sugars

Ingredients
2 pounds pork spare ribs, cut into 4 equal portions
1 tablespoon sea salt
1/2 teaspoon black pepper
1/2 teaspoon chili flakes
1 teaspoon cayenne pepper
1 teaspoon shallot powder
1 teaspoon garlic powder
1 teaspoon fennel seeds
1 tablespoon sugar
1 cup chicken stock
1 cup tomato ketchup
1/4 cup dark soy sauce

Directions
Generously sprinkle the pork spare ribs with all spices and sugar. Add the chicken stock andsecure the lid.

Choose the "Meat/Stew" mode and cook for 35 minutes at High pressure. Once cooking iscomplete, use a quick pressure release; carefully remove the lid.

Transfer the pork ribs to a baking pan. Mix the tomato ketchup and soy sauce; pour the mixtureover the pork ribs and roast in the preheated oven at 425 degrees F for 6 to 8 minutes. Bon appétit!

Country-Style Pork Meatballs

(Ready in about 20 minutes | Servings 4)

Per serving: 468 Calories; 24g Fat; 19.7g Carbs; 44.8g Protein; 6.2g Sugars

Ingredients
2 tablespoons vegetable oil
Meatballs:
1 ½ pounds ground pork
Kosher salt and ground black pepper, to your liking
1 teaspoon chili flakes
1 teaspoon mustard powder
1 egg
1/2 cup Parmesan, grated
2 bread slices, soaked in
4 tablespoons of milk
Marinara Sauce:
2 tablespoons olive oil
1 onion, chopped
3 cloves garlic, minced
1 tablespoon cayenne pepper
1 teaspoon maple syrup
2 large ripe tomatoes, crushed
1 teaspoon dried parsley flakes
1 cup water

Directions

Mix all ingredients for the meatballs until everything is well incorporated. Shape the mixture into small meatballs.

Press the "Sauté" button and heat 2 tablespoons of vegetable oil. Sear your meatballs until golden brown on all sides. Work in batches as needed. Reserve.

Press the "Sauté" button one more time; heat 2 tablespoons of olive oil. Cook the onion and garlic until tender and fragrant.

Now, add the remaining ingredients for the marinara sauce. Gently fold in the meatballs and secure the lid.

Spicy Sausage Bake

(Ready in about 20 minutes | Servings 4)

Per serving: 484 Calories; 41.8g Fat; 6.3g Carbs; 21.6g Protein; 4.1g Sugars

Ingredients
1 tablespoons canola oil
1 pound pork sausages, sliced
4 ounces streaky bacon
1 onion, sliced
4 garlic cloves, minced
1 bell pepper, sliced
1 red chili pepper, sliced
1 teaspoon brown sugar
1 teaspoon dried rosemary
1 teaspoon dried basil
Sea salt and freshly ground black pepper, to taste
2 tomatoes, pureed
1 cup chicken stock
1 cup white wine

Directions
Press the "Sauté" button and heat the oil. Sear the pork sausage until no longer pink. Add thebacon and cook until it is crisp.
Add a layer of onions and garlic; then, add the peppers. Sprinkle with sugar, rosemary, basil, saltand black pepper.
Add the tomatoes, chicken stock, and wine to the inner pot.
Secure the lid. Choose the "Manual" mode and cook for 10 minutes at High pressure. Oncecooking is complete, use a natural pressure release; carefully remove the lid. Bon appétit!

Beef

Ground Beef Sirloin Soup

(Ready in about 45 minutes | Servings 4)

Per serving: 276 Calories; 11.8g Fat; 22.6g Carbs; 19.3g Protein; 4.4g Sugars

Ingredients
1 tablespoon olive oil
1/2 pound beef sirloin, ground
1/2 teaspoon salt
1/2 teaspoon ground black pepper
4 cups bone broth
2 teaspoons dark soy sauce
1/2 cup shallots, chopped
1 teaspoon garlic, minced
2 carrots, chopped
2 Yukon Gold potatoes, chopped
1/2 cup tomato puree
2 bay leaves
1/2 teaspoon dried basil
1 teaspoon dried marjoram
1 teaspoon celery seeds

Directions
Press the "Sauté" button to heat up your Instant Pot. Heat the olive oil and brown the groundbeef sirloin, crumbling with a fork. Season with salt and black pepper.
Add the bone broth to deglaze the pot. Stir in the remaining ingredients.Secure the lid and choose the "Soup" button.
Cook for 30 minutes at High pressure. Once cooking is complete, use a natural release for 10minutes; carefully remove the lid. Bon appétit!

Sticky Beef with Brown Sauce

(Ready in about 40 minutes | Servings 4)

Per serving: 460 Calories; 18.7g Fat; 22.5g Carbs; 51.3g Protein; 15.7g Sugars

Ingredients
1 tablespoons olive oil
2 pounds beef stew meat, cubed
1/4 cup Syrah wine
1/2 cup dark brown sugar
6 cloves garlic, sliced
1 cup beef bone broth
1/4 cup soy sauce
1 teaspoon red pepper flakes
1 bay leaf
2 tablespoons arrowroot powder
1/4 cup scallions, roughly chopped

Directions
Press the "Sauté" button and heat the oil until sizzling. Then, brown the beef in batches.

Add a splash of red wine to deglaze the pot. Add the remaining wine, sugar, garlic, broth, soysauce, red pepper, and bay leaf.

Secure the lid. Choose the "Meat/Stew" mode and cook for 35 minutes at High pressure. Oncecooking is complete, use a quick pressure release; carefully remove the lid.

Press the "Sauté" button again and add the arrowroot powder. Let it cook until the sauce has reduced slightly and the flavors have concentrated. Serve garnished with fresh scallions andenjoy!

Hearty Ground Beef Frittata

(Ready in about 25 minutes | Servings 2)

Per serving: 368 Calories; 24.1g Fat; 3.7g Carbs; 33.9g Protein; 2.4g Sugars

Ingredients

1 tablespoon olive oil
1/2 pound ground chuck
4 eggs, whisked
A small bunch of green onions, chopped
1 small tomato, chopped
Sea salt and freshly ground black pepper, to your liking
1/2 teaspoon paprika
1/2 teaspoon garlic powder

Directions

Press the "Sauté" button to preheat your Instant Pot. Heat the oil and brown the beef for 2 to 3minutes, stirring continuously.
Lightly spritz a baking pan with cooking oil. Add all ingredients, including the browned beef tothe baking pan.
Cover with foil. Add 1 cup of water and a metal trivet to the Instant Pot. Lower the baking panonto the trivet.
Secure the lid. Choose the "Manual" mode and cook for 6 minutes at High pressure. Once cooking is complete, use a natural pressure release for 10 minutes; carefully remove the lid.
Slice in half and serve. Bon appétit!

Granny's Classic Beef and Gravy

(Ready in about 1 hour 15 minutes | Servings 6)

Per serving: 470 Calories; 8.8g Fat; 38.5g Carbs; 60.5g Protein; 2.6g Sugars

Ingredients

3 pounds top round roast
Sea salt and ground black pepper, to taste
1 teaspoon paprika
1 teaspoon dried rosemary
1 tablespoon lard, melted
1 ½ pounds fingerling potatoes
1 onion, thinly sliced
2 cloves garlic, smashed
1 bell pepper, deseeded and sliced
3 cups beef bone broth
1 ½ tablespoons potato starch

Directions

Toss the beef with the salt, black pepper, paprika, and rosemary until well coated on all sides.

Press the "Sauté" button to preheat your Instant Pot and melt the lard. Sear the beef for about 4minutes per side until it is browned.

Scatter the potatoes, onion, garlic, peppers around the top round roast. Add the beef bone broth.

Secure the lid. Choose the "Manual" mode and cook for 60 minutes at High pressure. Oncecooking is complete, use a natural pressure release for 10 minutes; carefully remove the lid.

Transfer the roast and vegetables to a serving platter; shred the roast with 2 forks. Mix the potato starch with 4 tablespoons of water. Press the "Sauté" button to preheat yourInstant Pot again. Once the liquid is boiling, add the slurry and let it cook until the gravy thickens.

Taste and adjust the seasonings. Serve warm.

———

Soups

Red Lentil and Spinach Soup

(Ready in about 10 minutes | Servings 5)

Per serving: 295 Calories; 1.9g Fat; 52.7g Carbs; 19.2g Protein; 1.6g Sugars

Ingredients

1 cups red lentils, rinsed

1 onion, chopped

2 cloves garlic, minced

1 teaspoon cumin

1 teaspoon smoked paprika

Sea salt and ground black pepper, to taste

2 carrots, sliced

6 cups water

2 bay leaves

2 cups fresh spinach leaves, torn into small pieces

Directions

Place all ingredients, except for the fresh spinach, in the inner pot.

Secure the lid. Choose the "Manual" mode and cook for 3 minutes at High pressure. Oncecooking is complete, use a quick pressure release; carefully remove the lid.

Stir in the spinach and seal the lid again; let it sit until the spinach just starts to wilt.Serve in individual bowls and enjoy!

Grandma's Noodle Soup

(Ready in about 20 minutes | Servings 6)

Per serving: 362 Calories; 25.4g Fat; 21.6g Carbs; 11.5g Protein; 2.9g Sugars

Ingredients
1 tablespoons olive oil
2 carrots, diced
2 parsnips, diced
1 yellow onion, chopped
2 cloves garlic, minced
6 cups chicken bone broth
1 bay leaf
Salt and freshly ground black pepper
2 pounds chicken thighs drumettes
2 cups wide egg noodles
1/4 cup fresh cilantro, roughly chopped

Directions
Press the "Sauté" button and heat the oil. Once hot, cook the carrots, parsnips, and onions untilthey are just tender.
Add the minced garlic and continue to cook for a minute more.
Add the chicken bone broth, bay leaf, salt, black pepper, and chicken to the inner pot.
Secure the lid. Choose the "Manual" mode and cook for 9 minutes at High pressure. Oncecooking is complete, use a quick pressure release; carefully remove the lid.
Shred the cooked chicken and set aside. Stir in noodles and press the "Sauté" button. Cookapproximately 5 minutes or until thoroughly heated.
Afterwards, add the chicken back into the soup. Serve garnished with fresh cilantro. Bon appétit!

Authentic French Onion Soup

(Ready in about 10 minutes | Servings 4)

Per serving: 325 Calories; 13.9g Fat; 31.7g Carbs; 19.2g Protein; 7.6g Sugars

Ingredients

4 tablespoons butter, melted
1 pound onions, thinly sliced
Kosher salt and ground white pepper, to taste
1/2 teaspoon dried sage
4 cups chicken bone broth1 loaf French bread, sliced
1 cup mozzarella cheese, shredded

Directions

Press the "Sauté" button and melt the butter. Once hot, cook the onions until golden andcaramelized.
Add the salt, pepper, sage, and chicken bone broth.
Secure the lid. Choose the "Manual" mode and cook for 2 minutes at High pressure. Oncecooking is complete, use a quick pressure release; carefully remove the lid.
Divide the soup between four oven safe bowls; top with the bread and shredded cheese; now, place the bowls under the broiler for about 4 minutes or until the cheese has melted. Bon appétit!

Creamed Corn and Chicken Soup

(Ready in about 20 minutes | Servings 6)

Per serving: 313 Calories; 15.5g Fat; 19.4g Carbs; 24.7g Protein; 4.6g Sugars

Ingredients

1 tablespoon olive oil
1 yellow onion, chopped
1 celery stalk, diced
1 carrot, finely diced
1 turnip, diced
6 cups roasted vegetable broth
1 pound chicken breasts, skinless, boneless and diced
1 teaspoon garlic powder
1 teaspoon mustard powder
1 (15-ounce) can creamed corn
4 large eggs, whisked
Kosher salt and ground black pepper, to taste

Directions

Press the "Sauté" button and heat the oil. Now, sauté the onion until just tender and translucent.Add the celery, carrot, turnip, vegetable broth, chicken, garlic powder, and mustard powder.

Secure the lid. Choose the "Manual" mode and cook for 9 minutes at High pressure. Oncecooking is complete, use a quick pressure release; carefully remove the lid.

Press the "Sauté" button and use the lowest setting. Stir in the creamed corn and eggs; let itsimmer, stirring continuously for about 5 minutes or until everything is thoroughly heated.

Season with salt and pepper to taste and serve warm. Bon appétit!

Stews

Northern Italian Beef Stew

(Ready in about 35 minutes | Servings 6)

Per serving: 434 Calories; 16.6g Fat; 29.5g Carbs; 40.7g Protein; 6.1g Sugars

Ingredients

1 pounds beef top round, cut into bite-sized chunks
1/4 cup all-purpose flour
1 tablespoon Italian seasoning
Sea salt and ground black pepper, to taste
1 tablespoon lard, at room temperature
1 onion, chopped
4 cloves garlic, pressed
1/4 cup cooking wine
1/4 cup tomato paste
1 pound sweet potatoes, diced
1/2 pound carrots, sliced into rounds
2 bell peppers, deveined and sliced
1 teaspoon fish sauce
2 bay leaves
4 cups beef broth
2 tablespoons fresh Italian parsley, roughly chopped

Directions

Toss the beef chunks with the flour, Italian seasoning, salt, and pepper until well coated. Press the "Sauté" button and melt the lard; brown the beef chunks on all sides, stirringfrequently; reserve. Then, sauté the onion and garlic for a minute or so; add the wine and stir, scraping up anybrowned bits from the bottom of the inner pot.

Add the beef back into the inner pot. Stir in the tomato paste, sweet potatoes, carrots, bellpeppers, fish sauce, bay leaves, and beef broth. Secure the lid. Choose the "Meat/Stew" mode and cook for 20 minutes at High pressure. Oncecooking is complete, use a natural pressure release for 10 minutes; carefully remove the lid. Serve garnished with Italian parsley.

Italian Beef Ragù

(Ready in about 20 minutes | Servings 5)

Per serving: 475 Calories; 40.6g Fat; 6.1g Carbs; 20.7g Protein; 2.5g Sugars

Ingredients
1 tablespoons butter, melted
1 medium leek, diced
2 carrots, diced
1 stalk celery, diced
5 ounces bacon, diced
1 pound ground chuck
1/2 cup Italian red wine
1/4 cup tomato puree
2 cups chicken stock
1 tablespoon Italian seasoning blend
1/2 teaspoon kosher salt
1/2 teaspoon black pepper

Directions
Press the "Sauté" button and melt the butter. Sauté the leek, carrot, celery and garlic for 2 to 3minutes.
Add the bacon and ground beef to the inner pot; continue to cook an additional 3 minutes,stirring frequently. Add the remaining ingredients to the inner pot.
Secure the lid. Choose the "Manual" mode and cook for 5 minutes at High pressure. Oncecooking is complete, use a quick pressure release; carefully remove the lid.
Serve with hot pasta if desired. Bon appétit!

Rich and Easy Chicken Purloo

(Ready in about 25 minutes | Servings 8)

Per serving: 407 Calories; 9.4g Fat; 40.9g Carbs; 36.5g Protein; 1.7g Sugars

Ingredients
1 tablespoon olive oil
1 onion, chopped
3 pounds chicken legs, boneless and skinless
2 garlic cloves, minced
5 cups water
2 carrots, diced
2 celery ribs, diced
2 bay leaves
1 teaspoon mustard seeds
1/4 teaspoon marjoram
Seasoned salt and freshly ground black pepper, to taste
1 teaspoon cayenne pepper
2 cups white long-grain rice

Directions
Press the "Sauté" button and heat the olive oil. Now, add the onion and chicken legs; cook untilthe onion is translucent or about 4 minutes. Stir in the minced garlic and continue to cook for a minute more. Add the water.
Secure the lid. Choose the "Manual" mode and cook for 10 minutes at High pressure. Oncecooking is complete, use a quick pressure release; carefully remove the lid.
Add the remaining ingredients.
Secure the lid. Choose the "Manual" mode and cook for 5 minutes at High pressure. Oncecooking is complete, use a quick pressure release; carefully remove the lid. Serve warm.

Seafood and Vegetable Ragout

(Ready in about 20 minutes | Servings 4)

Per serving: 312 Calories; 11.9g Fat; 15.9g Carbs; 36.6g Protein; 5g
Sugars

Ingredients
1 tablespoons olive oil
1 shallot, diced
2 carrots, diced
1 parsnip, diced
1 teaspoon fresh garlic, minced
1/2 cup dry white wine
2 cups fish stock
1 tomato, pureed
1 bay leaf
1 pound shrimp, deveined
1/2 pound scallops
Seasoned salt and freshly ground pepper, to taste
1 tablespoon paprika
2 tablespoons fresh parsley, chopped
1 lime, sliced

Directions
Press the "Sauté" button and heat the oil. Now, sauté the shallot,
carrot, and parsnip for 4 to 5minutes or until they are tender.
Stir in the garlic and continue to sauté an additional 30 second or until
aromatic.
Stir in the white wine, stock, tomato, bay leaf, shrimp, scallops, salt,
black pepper, and paprika.
Secure the lid. Choose the "Manual" mode. Cook for 5 minutes at High
pressure. Once cookingis complete, use a natural pressure release for 5
minutes; carefully remove the lid. Serve garnished with fresh parsley
and lime slices. Enjoy!

Stocks and Sauces

Classic Fish Stock

(Ready in about 55 minutes | Servings 8)

Per serving: 63 Calories; 3.5g Fat; 2.7g Carbs; 4.9g Protein; 1.3g Sugars

Ingredients
1 pounds meaty bones and heads of halibut, washed
2 lemongrass stalks, chopped
2 carrots, chopped
1 parsnip, chopped
1 onion, quartered
2 sprigs rosemary
2 sprigs thyme
2 tablespoons olive oil

Directions
Place all ingredients in the inner pot. Add cold water until the pot is 2/3 full.
Secure the lid. Choose the "Soup/Broth" mode and cook for 40 minutes at High pressure. Oncecooking is complete, use a natural pressure release for 10 minutes; carefully remove the lid.
Strain the vegetables and fish. Bon appétit!

Roasted Vegetable Stock

(Ready in about 1 hour 15 minutes | Servings 10)

Per serving: 56 Calories; 3.4g Fat; 3.2g Carbs; 0.3g Protein; 1.4g Sugars

Ingredients

4 carrots, cut into 2-inch pieces
4 medium celery ribs, cut into 2-inch pieces
2 onions, peeled and quartered
2 sprigs fresh rosemary
2 sprigs fresh thyme
3 tablespoons olive oil
Kosher salt and black peppercorns, to taste
1 cup dry white wine
10 cups water

Directions

Start by preheating your oven to 400 degrees F. Grease a large roasting
pan with cooking spray
Place the carrots, celery, onions, and herbs in the prepared roasting pan.
Roast, tossing halfwaythrough the cooking time, until the vegetables are
tender about 35 minutes.
Transfer the vegetables to the inner pot. Add the remaining ingredients.
Secure the lid. Choose the "Soup/Broth" mode and cook for 30
minutes at High pressure. Oncecooking is complete, use a natural
pressure release for 10 minutes; carefully remove the lid.
Strain the broth through a fine-mesh sieve and discard the solids. Let it
cool completely beforestoring.

Spanish Chorizo Sauce

(Ready in about 20 minutes | Servings 4)

Per serving: 385 Calories; 24.9g Fat; 20.2g Carbs; 21.1g Protein; 11.1g
Sugars

Ingredients
1 tablespoon olive oil
1 pound Chorizo sausage, sliced
1 onion, chopped
1 teaspoon garlic, minced
1 sweet pepper, seeded and finely chopped
1 habanero pepper, seeded and minced
2 tablespoons sugar
1 teaspoon dried basil
1 teaspoon dried rosemary
1 teaspoon red pepper flakes
Sea salt and freshly ground black pepper, to taste
1 (28-ounce) can diced tomatoes, with juice
1 cup chicken broth

Directions
Press the "Sauté" button and heat the oil. When the oil starts to sizzle,
cook the Chorizo until nolonger pink; crumble it with a wooden
spatula.
Add the onion, garlic, and peppers and cook for a minute or so. Add a
splash of chicken broth todeglaze the pan.
Stir in the remaining ingredients.
Secure the lid. Choose the "Manual" mode and cook for 6 minutes at
High pressure. Once cooking is complete, use a natural pressure release
for 10 minutes; carefully remove the lid. Bonappétit!

Simple Court Bouillon

(Ready in about 45 minutes | Servings 8)

Per serving: 55 Calories; 3.4g Fat; 1.6g Carbs; 0.1g Protein; 0.6g Sugars

Ingredients

1 tablespoon salt
1 teaspoon mixed peppercorns
1 cup white wine
2 onions, sliced
2 celery ribs, sliced
2 carrots, sliced
2 bay leaves
2 sprig fresh rosemary
A bunch of fresh parsley
1 lemon, sliced
2 tablespoons olive oil

Directions

Add all ingredients to the inner pot of your Instant Pot. Add cold water until the inner pot is 2/3full.
Secure the lid. Choose the "Soup/Broth" mode and cook for 30 minutes at High pressure. Oncecooking is complete, use a natural pressure release for 10 minutes; carefully remove the lid.
Discard the vegetables. Bon appétit!

Fish and Seafood

Tilapia Fillets with Cremini Mushrooms

(Ready in about 15 minutes | Servings 3)

Per serving: 218 Calories; 12.9g Fat; 2.2g Carbs; 23.6g Protein; 0.7g Sugars

Ingredients

3 tilapia fillets
1/2 teaspoon sea salt
Freshly ground black pepper, to taste
1 teaspoon cayenne pepper
1 cup Cremini mushrooms, thinly sliced
1/2 cup yellow onions, sliced
2 cloves garlic, peeled and minced
2 sprigs thyme, leaves picked
2 sprigs rosemary, leaves picked
2 tablespoons avocado oil

Directions

Season the tilapia fillets with salt, black pepper, and cayenne pepper on all sides. Place the tilapiafillets in the steaming basket fitted for your Instant Pot.
Place the sliced mushroom and yellow onions on top of the fillets. Add the garlic, thyme, androsemary; drizzle avocado oil over everything.
Add 1 ½ cups of water to the base of your Instant Pot. Add the steaming basket to the Instant Potand secure the lid.
Select the "Manual" mode. Cook for 8 minutes at Low pressure.
Once cooking is complete, use a quick release; remove the lid carefully. Serve immediately.

Saucy Parmesan Cod with Basmati Rice

(Ready in about 15 minutes | Servings 4)

Per serving: 443 Calories; 25.4g Fat; 33.7g Carbs; 36.9g Protein; 1.1g Sugars

Ingredients
2 cups basmati rice
2 cups water
¼ pounds cod, slice into small pieces
1 Salt and ground black pepper, to taste
1 teaspoon paprika
2 bay leaves
1 teaspoon coriander
1 teaspoon lemon thyme
2 tablespoons lemon juice
1/2 cup heavy cream
1 cup Parmesan cheese, freshly grated

Directions
Choose the "Manual" button and cook the basmati rice with water for 4 minutes. Once cookingis complete, use a natural release; carefully remove the lid. Reserve.

Now, press the "Sauté" button on your Instant Pot. Add the remaining ingredients and cook untilthe Parmesan has melted.

Serve the fish mixture over the hot basmati rice and enjoy!

Sausage and Prawn Boil with Old Bay Sauce

(Ready in about 15 minutes | Servings 4)

Per serving: 441 Calories; 28.6g Fat; 14.5g Carbs; 32.4g Protein; 1.6g Sugars

Ingredients
1/2 pound beef sausage, sliced
4 baby potatoes
1 cup fume (fish stock)
1/4 cup butter
2 cloves garlic, minced
1 teaspoon Old Bay seasoning
1/4 teaspoon Tabasco sauce
Sea salt and white pepper, to taste
1 pound prawns
1 fresh lemon, juiced

Directions
Place the sausage and potatoes in the inner pot; cover with the fish stock.

Secure the lid. Choose the "Manual" mode and cook for 5 minutes at High pressure. Once cooking is complete, use a quick pressure release; carefully remove the lid. Reserve. Clean theinner pot.

Press the "Sauté" button and melt the butter. Once hot, sauté the minced garlic until aromatic or about 1 minute. Stir in the Old Bay seasoning, Tabasco, salt, and white pepper. Lastly, stir in theprawns. Continue to simmer for 1 to 2 minutes or until the shrimp turn pink. Press the "Cancel" button.Add the sausages and potatoes, drizzle lemon juice over the top and serve warm.

Spicy Thai Prawns

(Ready in about 10 minutes | Servings 4)

Per serving: 283 Calories; 11.1g Fat; 12.3g Carbs; 32.7g Protein; 7.4g Sugars

Ingredients
2 tablespoons coconut oil
1 small white onion, chopped
2 cloves garlic, minced
1 ½ pounds prawns, deveined
1/2 teaspoon red chili flakes
1 bell pepper, seeded and sliced
1 cup coconut milk
2 tablespoons fish sauce
2 tablespoons lime juice
1 tablespoon sugar
Kosher salt and white pepper, to your liking
1/2 teaspoon cayenne pepper
1 teaspoon fresh ginger, ground
2 tablespoons fresh cilantro, roughly chopped

Directions
Press the "Sauté" button and heat the coconut oil; once hot, sauté the onion and garlic untilaromatic.
Add the prawns, red chili flakes, bell pepper, coconut milk, fish sauce, lime juice, sugar, salt,white pepper, cayenne pepper, and ginger.
Secure the lid. Choose the "Manual" mode and cook for 3 minutes at Low pressure. Oncecooking is complete, use a quick pressure release; carefully remove the lid.
Divide between serving bowls and serve garnished with fresh cilantro. Enjoy!

Beans – Pasta - Grains

Bulgur Wheat with Pico de Gallo

(Ready in about 25 minutes | Servings 4)

Per serving: 184 Calories; 10.4g Fat; 17.8g Carbs; 6g Protein; 3.8g Sugars

Ingredients
2 tablespoons vegetable oil
1 yellow onion, chopped
2 garlic cloves, minced
1 ¼ cups bulgur wheat
3 cups roasted vegetable broth
Sea salt and white pepper, to taste
1 teaspoon smoked paprika
1/2 cup Pico de gallo

Directions
Press the "Sauté" button to preheat your Instant Pot. Now, sauté the onions with garlic for 1minute or so.
Then, stir the bulgur wheat, broth, salt, pepper, and paprika into your Instant Pot.
Secure the lid. Choose the "Manual" mode and High pressure; cook for 12 minutes. Once cooking is complete, use a natural pressure release for 10 minutes; carefully remove the lid.
Serve topped with chilled Pico de gallo. Bon appétit!

Oatmeal with Bananas and Walnuts

(Ready in about 25 minutes | Servings 4)

Per serving: 244 Calories; 10.1g Fat; 48.4g Carbs; 10.4g Protein; 9.2g Sugars

Ingredients

1 cups steel cut oats
5 ½ cups water
1/2 teaspoon ground cinnamon
1/4 teaspoon cardamom
1/4 teaspoon grated nutmeg
2 bananas
1/2 cup walnuts, chopped

Directions

Add the steel cut oats to your Instant Pot. Pour in the water. Add the cinnamon, cardamom, andnutmeg.

Secure the lid. Choose the "Manual" mode and cook for 10 minutes under High pressure.

Once cooking is complete, use a natural release for 10 minutes; remove the lid carefully. Ladleinto serving bowls.

Top with bananas and walnuts. Bon appétit!

Grandmother's Buttermilk Cornbread

(Ready in about 1 hour | Servings 8)

Per serving: 208 Calories; 7.8g Fat; 31.3g Carbs; 3.6g Protein; 7.7g Sugars

Ingredients

1 cup yellow cornmeal1 cup all-purpose flour
1 tablespoon baking powder
1/2 cup granulated sugar
A pinch of salt
A pinch of grated nutmeg
1 cup buttermilk
1/4 cup safflower oil

Directions

Add 1 cup of water and metal rack to the inner pot. Spritz a baking pan with cooking oil.

Thoroughly combine the cornmeal, flour, baking powder, sugar, salt, and grated nutmeg. Inanother mixing bowl, whisk buttermilk with safflower oil.

Add the wet mixture to the cornmeal mixture. Scrape the mixture into the prepared baking pan.Cover with a sheet of greased aluminum foil. Lower the pan onto the rack.

Secure the lid. Choose the "Manual" mode and cook for 55 minutes at High pressure. Oncecooking is complete, use a quick pressure release; carefully remove the lid.

Place the cornbread on a cooling rack before slicing and serving. Bon appétit!

Millet Porridge with Almonds and Raisins

(Ready in about 25 minutes | Servings 5)

Per serving: 372 Calories; 10.1g Fat; 60.6g Carbs; 10.6g Protein; 10.7g Sugars

Ingredients

1 ½ cups millet
3 cups water
1/2 cup golden raisins
1/4 cup almonds, roughly chopped
1 tablespoon orange juice
A pinch of sea salt

Directions

Place all ingredients in the inner pot of your Instant Pot and close the lid.

Secure the lid. Choose the "Manual" mode and cook for 12 minutes at High pressure. Oncecooking is complete, use a natural pressure release for 10 minutes; carefully remove the lid.

Taste and adjust the seasonings. Bon appétit!

Low Carb

Bacon Frittata Muffins

(Ready in about 15 minutes | Servings 6)

Per serving: 226 Calories; 20.1g Fat; 2.3g Carbs; 9.3g Protein; 1.3g Sugars

Ingredients

6 thin meaty bacon slices
1 large-sized zucchini, grated
1 red bell pepper, chopped
1 green bell pepper, chopped
4 teaspoons butter, melted
1/2 cup Colby cheese, shredded
3 egg, beaten
2 tablespoons cream cheese, room temperature
1 teaspoon shallot powder
1/2 teaspoon dried dill weed
1/2 teaspoon cayenne pepper
Salt and black pepper, to taste

Directions

Start by adding 1 ½ cups of water and a metal trivet to the bottom of your Instant Pot.Place the bacon slices in 6 silicone cupcake liners. Add the zucchini and bell peppers.

Now, mix the butter, Colby cheese, eggs, cream cheese, shallot powder, dried dill weed, cayennepepper, salt, and black pepper. Spoon this mixture into the liners.

Put the liners into an oven-safe bowl. Cover with a piece of foil. Lower the bowl onto the trivet.

Secure the lid. Choose "Manual" mode and High pressure; cook for 10 minutes. Once cooking iscomplete, use a natural pressure release; carefully remove the lid. Bon appétit!

Greek-Style Mushroom Muffins

(Ready in about 10 minutes | Servings 6)

Per serving: 259 Calories; 18.9g Fat; 6.7g Carbs; 15.7g Protein; 3.9g Sugars

Ingredients
6 eggs
1 red onion, chopped
2 cups button mushrooms, chopped
Sea salt and ground black pepper, to taste
1 ½ cups Feta cheese, shredded
1/2 cup Kalamata olives, pitted and sliced

Directions
Start by adding 1 ½ cups of water and a metal rack to the bottom of the Instant Pot. Spritz eachmuffin liner with a nonstick cooking spray.
In a mixing bowl, thoroughly combine the eggs, onions, mushrooms, salt, and black pepper.Now, pour this mixture into the muffin liners.
Secure the lid. Choose "Manual" mode and Low pressure; cook for 7 minutes. Once cooking iscomplete, use a quick pressure release; carefully remove the lid.
Sprinkle the cheese and olives on top of the cups; cover with the lid for a few minutes to allow itto melt. Enjoy!

Zucchini Cardamom Bread

(Ready in about 35 minutes | Servings 8)

Per serving: 205 Calories; 19.1g Fat; 4.3g Carbs; 6.1g Protein; 0.9g Sugars

Ingredients
4 eggs
1/3 cup olive oil
1 cup almond flour
2 tablespoons coconut flour
1 teaspoon stevia, liquid
A pinch of salt
A pinch of grated nutmeg
1 teaspoon baking powder
1 teaspoon ground cardamom
1 cup zucchini, grated

Directions
Prepare the Instant Pot by adding 1 ½ cups of water and a metal rack to its bottom. Lightly grease a baking pan with a nonstick cooking spray.
In a mixing dish, thoroughly combine the dry ingredients. Then, in another bowl, thoroughly combine the wet ingredients.
Add the wet mixture to the dry mixture; continue to mix until uniform, creamy and smooth. Pour the batter into the prepared pan.
Lower the pan onto the trivet.
Secure the lid. Choose "Bean/Chili" mode and High pressure; cook for 25 minutes. Once cooking is complete, use a natural pressure release; carefully remove the lid.
Allow the zucchini bread to cool completely before cutting and serving. Bon appétit!

Cauliflower Breakfast Cups

(Ready in about 15 minutes | Servings 6)

Per serving: 335 Calories; 25.9g Fat; 5.8g Carbs; 19.8g Protein; 2.6g Sugars

Ingredients
1/2 pound cauliflower, riced
Sea salt and ground black pepper, to taste
1/2 teaspoon cayenne pepper
1/2 teaspoon dried dill weed
1/2 teaspoon dried basil
1/4 teaspoon dried oregano
2 tablespoons olive oil
2 garlic cloves, minced
1/2 cup scallions, chopped
1 cup Romano cheese, preferably freshly grated
Salt and ground black pepper, to taste
7 eggs, beaten
1/2 cup Cotija cheese, grated

Directions
Start by adding 1 ½ cups of water and a metal rack to the bottom of the Instant Pot. Spritz eachmuffin cup with a nonstick cooking spray.
Mix the ingredients until everything is well incorporated.
Now, spoon the mixture into lightly greased muffin cups. Lower the cups onto the rack in theInstant Pot.
Secure the lid. Choose "Manual" mode and High pressure; cook for 10 minutes. Once cooking iscomplete, use a natural pressure release; carefully remove the lid. Bon appétit!

Vegan

Traditional Russian Borscht

(Ready in about 15 minutes | Servings 4)

Per serving: 183 Calories; 7.3g Fat; 22.5g Carbs; 8.4g Protein; 7.7g Sugars

Ingredients

1 ½ tablespoons olive oil
1/2 cup onions, chopped
2 garlic cloves, pressed
Kosher salt and ground black pepper, to taste
1/2 pound potatoes, peeled and diced
2 carrots, chopped
1/2 pound beets, peeled and coarsely shredded
2 tablespoons red-wine vinegar
1 tomato, chopped
4 cups vegetable stock
1/2 teaspoon caraway seeds
1/4 cup fresh dill, roughly chopped

Directions

Press the "Sauté" button to preheat your Instant Pot. Heat the oil and cook the onions and garlicuntil tender and fragrant.
Add the remaining ingredients, except for the fresh dill.
Secure the lid. Choose the "Manual" mode and cook for 10 minutes under High pressure. Oncecooking is complete, use a natural release; carefully remove the lid.
Serve the soup with chopped fresh dill. Enjoy!

Purple Cabbage with Basmati Rice

(Ready in about 25 minutes | Servings 4)

Per serving: 242 Calories; 13.3g Fat; 35.2g Carbs; 7.8g Protein; 10g Sugars

Ingredients
1 tablespoons olive oil
2 shallots, diced
1 garlic clove, minced
1 head purple cabbage, cut into wedges
2 ripe tomatoes, pureed
2 tablespoons tomato ketchup
1 cup basmati rice
1 ½ cups water
1 bay leaf
1/4 teaspoon marjoram
1/2 teaspoon cayenne pepper
Salt and freshly ground black pepper, to taste
1/4 cup fresh chives, chopped

Directions
Press the "Sauté" button to preheat the Instant Pot. Heat the olive oil and sauté the shallots untilthey are just tender.

Now, stir in the minced garlic and cook until it is lightly browned and aromatic.

Stir in the cabbage, tomatoes, ketchup, rice, water, bay leaf, marjoram, cayenne pepper, salt, andblack pepper.

Secure the lid. Select the "Manual" mode and cook for 6 minutes under High pressure. Once cooking is complete, use a natural release for 15 minutes; remove the lid carefully. Serve warmgarnished with fresh chopped chives. Bon appétit!

Quinoa and Chickpea Bowl

(Ready in about 10 minutes | Servings 4)

Per serving: 392 Calories; 8.1g Fat; 66.9g Carbs; 15.5g Protein; 7.9g
Sugars

Ingredients

1 teaspoons sesame oil
1 shallot, thinly sliced
2 bell peppers, thinly sliced
1 jalapeño pepper, seeded and sliced
1 teaspoon garlic, minced
Sea salt and ground black pepper, to taste
1/2 teaspoon mustard powder
1 teaspoon fennel seeds
1/2 teaspoon ground cumin
1 ½ cups quinoa, rinsed
1 ½ cups water
1 cup tomato purée
1 (15-ounce) can chickpeas, drained and rinsed
1 lime, cut into wedges

Directions

Press the "Sauté" button to preheat your Instant Pot. Heat the sesame
oil. Then, sweat the shallotand peppers until they are tender and
fragrant.

Now, add the garlic, salt, black pepper, mustard powder, fennel seeds,
cumin, quinoa, water,tomato purée, and chickpeas.

Secure the lid. Choose the "Manual" mode and High pressure; cook for
1 minute. Once cookingis complete, use a natural pressure release;
carefully remove the lid.

Serve with fresh lime wedges. Bon appétit!

Great Northern Beans on Toast
(Ready in about 35 minutes | Servings 6)

Per serving: 393 Calories; 6.5g Fat; 67.4g Carbs; 18.4g Protein; 16.8g Sugars

Ingredients
1 cups Great Northern beans
1 red onion, peeled and chopped
1 cup water
2 cups vegetable broth
1/2 cup ketchup Garlic salt, to taste
1 teaspoon chili powder
1/2 teaspoon mixed peppercorns, crushed
1/4 cup dark brown sugar
2 cloves garlic, minced
2 sprigs fresh sage, roughly chopped
2 tablespoons canola oil
6 slices sourdough bread, toasted

Directions
Add the beans, onion, water, and broth to the Instant Pot.
Secure the lid. Choose the "Soup" mode and High pressure; cook for 25 minutes. Once cookingis complete, use a natural pressure release; carefully remove the lid.
Add the ketchup, salt, chili powder, mixed peppercorns, sugar, garlic, sage, and oil. Press the"Sauté" button.
Let it simmer an additional 5 to 7 minutes or until everything is heated through. Spoon the hotbeans over the toasted bread and serve immediately.

Vegetable and Side Dishes

Vegan Baked Beans

(Ready in about 1 hour 10 minutes | Servings 6)

Per serving: 594 Calories; 5.6g Fat; 114g Carbs; 26.2g Protein; 51.4g Sugars

Ingredients

1 ½ pounds pinto beans, rinsed and drained
8 cups water
2 tablespoons olive oil
2 onions, chopped
5 cloves garlic, minced
1 cup molasses
1 cup ketchup
1 teaspoon salt
2 tablespoons soy sauce
1 tablespoon
Cholula hot sauce

Directions

Place the beans and water in your Instant Pot.
Secure the lid. Choose the "Bean/Chili" mode and cook for 40 minutes at High pressure. Once cooking is complete, use a natural pressure release for 10 minutes; carefully remove the lid. Setaside.
Press the "Sauté" button and heat the oil until sizzling. Now, cook the onion and garlic untiltender and fragrant. Add the reserved beans back to the inner pot. Stir in the remaining ingredients.
Secure the lid. Choose the "Manual" mode and cook for 10 minutes at High pressure. Oncecooking is complete, use a quick pressure release.
Bon appétit!

Punjabi Bean Curry

(Ready in about 35 minutes | Servings 5)

Per serving: 406 Calories; 6.2g Fat; 66g Carbs; 24.5g Protein; 1.1g Sugars

Ingredients
1 pound red kidney beans
8 cups water
2 tablespoons canola oil
1 onion, finely sliced
1 teaspoon ginger garlic paste
1/4 teaspoon red curry paste
2 small-sized potatoes, peeled and diced
1 green chili pepper, finely chopped
Sea salt and freshly ground black pepper, to taste
1/2 teaspoon turmeric powder
1/2 teaspoon avocado powder
2 tomatoes, pureed
1 tablespoon fenugreek, chopped

Directions
Add the red kidney beans and water to the inner pot of your Instant Pot. Secure the lid. Choose the "Bean/Chili" mode and cook for 25 minutes at High pressure. Oncecooking is complete, use a quick pressure release; carefully remove the lid. Drain and reserve.
Press the "Sauté" button and heat the oil until sizzling. Now, sauté the onion until tender andtranslucent. Add the remaining ingredients. Gently stir to combine. Secure the lid. Choose the "Manual" mode and cook for 4 minutes at High pressure. Oncecooking is complete, use a quick pressure release; carefully remove the lid. Stir the reserved beans into the potato mixture and serve warm. Bon appétit!

Parmesan Brussels Sprouts
(Ready in about 15 minutes | Servings 6)

Per serving: 184 Calories; 15.8g Fat; 10.1g Carbs; 3.9g Protein; 2.5g Sugars

Ingredients
1 ½ pounds Brussels sprouts, trimmed and halved
1 stick butter
1/2 teaspoon basil
1 teaspoon rosemary
1 teaspoon garlic, minced
1 teaspoon shallot powder
Sea salt and red pepper, to taste

Directions
Place 1 cup of water and a steamer basket in the inner pot of your Instant Pot. Place the Brusselssprouts in the steamer basket.
Secure the lid. Choose the "Steam" mode and cook for 3 minutes at High pressure. Once cookingis complete, use a quick pressure release; carefully remove the lid.
Press the "Sauté" button and melt the butter; once hot, cook the basil, rosemary, and garlic for 40seconds or until aromatic.
Add in the Brussels sprouts, shallot powder, salt, and pepper. Press the "Cancel" button. Scatterthe grated parmesan cheese over the Brussels sprouts and serve immediately. Bon appétit!

Aromatic Snow Peas
(Ready in about 10 minutes | Servings 4)

Per serving: 126 Calories; 5.4g Fat; 16.9g Carbs; 3.6g Protein; 8.1g Sugars

Ingredients
1 ½ tablespoons coconut oil
1 pound snow peas, frozen
2 carrots, sliced
1 parsnip, sliced Seasoned salt, to taste
1 cup water
1/2 teaspoon ground black pepper
1/2 teaspoon red pepper flakes, crushed
1 tablespoon white sugar

Directions
Add all of the above ingredients to your Instant Pot.
Secure the lid. Select the "Steam" setting; cook for 4 minutes at High pressure. Once cooking iscomplete, use a quick pressure release; carefully remove the lid.
Transfer everything to a serving dish. Enjoy!

Rice

Mexican-Style Salsa Rice

(Ready in about 35 minutes | Servings 4)

Per serving: 408 Calories; 15.6g Fat; 40.7g Carbs; 25.7g Protein; 3.2g Sugars

Ingredients
1 cup brown rice
1 cup chicken broth
1 cup chunky salsa
1 cup Cotija cheese, shredded

Directions
Add the brown rice, chicken broth, salsa, oregano, salt, and black pepper to the inner pot.
Secure the lid. Choose the "Manual" mode and cook for 22 minutes at High pressure. Oncecooking is complete, use a natural pressure release for 10 minutes; carefully remove the lid.
Divide between serving bowls and serve with shredded cheese. Enjoy!

Pulao Rice Pakistani Style

(Ready in about 30 minutes | Servings 4)

Per serving: 392 Calories; 7.3g Fat; 72.2g Carbs; 9.2g Protein; 0.9g Sugars

Ingredients

1 tablespoons ghee
1 shallot, chopped
2 garlic cloves, minced
1 ½ cups basmati rice, rinsed
2 cups vegetable broth
Sea salt and white pepper, to taste
1 teaspoon coriander seeds
2 black cardamoms
2 green cardamoms
2 tez patta (bay leaf)
1 teaspoon turmeric powder
1 cup sweet corn kernels, thawed

Directions

Press the "Sauté" button and melt the ghee. Once hot, cook the shallot for 4 minutes or until justtender and fragrant. Stir in the garlic and cook an additional minute or until aromatic.

Now, add the basmati rice, broth, and spices.

Secure the lid. Choose the "Manual" mode and cook for 4 minutes at High pressure. Once cooking is complete, use a natural pressure release for 15 minutes; carefully remove the lid.

Add the sweet corn kernels and seal the lid again. Let it sit in the residual heat until thoroughlyheated. Enjoy!

Chicken, Broccoli and Rice Casserole

(Ready in about 30 minutes | Servings 4)

Per serving: 563 Calories; 21.2g Fat; 56.5g Carbs; 36.5g Protein; 6.7g Sugars

Ingredients

3 tablespoons butter, melted
1 chicken breast, skinless
1 shallot, sliced
1 teaspoon garlic, minced1 pound broccoli florets
1 cup white rice
1 cup tomato puree
2 cups chicken broth
1 teaspoon paprika
1 teaspoon Italian seasoning blend
Kosher salt and freshly ground pepper, to taste
5 ounces cheddar cheese, shredded

Directions

Press the "Sauté" button and melt 1 tablespoon of butter. Once hot, cook the chicken breast untilit is golden brown on both sides.
Shred the chicken with two forks. Add it back to the inner pot. Add the shallots, garlic, broccoli,rice, tomato puree, and chicken broth; stir in the remaining butter.
Season with the paprika, Italian seasonings, salt, and black pepper.
Secure the lid. Choose the "Rice" mode and cook for 10 minutes at Low pressure. Once cookingis complete, use a natural pressure release for 10 minutes; carefully remove the lid.
Top with cheese. Seal the lid again and let it sit in the residual heat until the cheese melts. Serveimmediately.

Perfect Sushi Rice

(Ready in about 30 minutes | Servings 4)

Per serving: 291 Calories; 1.9g Fat; 60.7g Carbs; 5.1g Protein; 3.5g Sugars

Ingredients
1 ½ cups sushi rice, rinsed
1 ½ cups water
1/4 cup rice vinegar
1 tablespoon brown sugar
1/2 teaspoon salt
2 tablespoons soy sauce

Directions
Place the sushi rice and water in the inner pot of your Instant Pot. Secure the lid. Choose the "Rice" mode and cook for 10 minutes at Low pressure. Once cookingis complete, use a natural pressure release for 15 minutes; carefully remove the lid.
Meanwhile, whisk the rice vinegar, sugar, salt and soy sauce in a mixing dish; microwave thesauce for 1 minute.
Pour the sauce over the sushi rice; stir to combine. Assemble your sushi rolls and enjoy!

Snacks and Appetizers

Ranch-Style Popcorn

(Ready in about 10 minutes | Servings 6)

Per serving: 177 Calories; 13.9g Fat; 11.1g Carbs; 2.4g Protein; 3.5g Sugars

Ingredients
2 tablespoons olive oil
3/4 cup corn kernels
4 tablespoons butter
1-ounce packet ranch seasoning mix
Sea salt, to taste

Directions
Press the "Sauté" button to preheat your Instant Pot.
Now, heat the olive oil; add corn kernels. Sauté until the corn kernels are well coated with oil.
Secure the lid and choose the "Manual" function; cook for 5 minutes at High pressure. Oncecooking is complete, use a quick release; carefully remove the lid.
In a saucepan, melt the butter with ranch seasoning mix. Lastly, toss the ranch butter withpopcorn; season with salt. Enjoy!

Chinese Sticky Baby Carrots

(Ready in about 10 minutes | Servings 6)

Per serving: 110 Calories; 4.5g Fat; 17.2g Carbs; 2.3g Protein; 8.1g Sugars

Ingredients
1 pounds baby carrots, trimmed and scrubbed
1/2 cup orange juice
1/2 cup water
2 tablespoons raisins
2 tablespoons soy sauce
2 tablespoons Shaoxing wine
1 teaspoon garlic powder
1/2 teaspoon shallot powder
1 teaspoon mustard powder
1/4 teaspoon cumin seeds
2 teaspoons butter, at room temperature
2 tablespoons sesame seeds, toasted

Directions
Place all ingredients, except for the sesame seeds, in the inner pot of your Instant Pot.
Secure the lid. Choose the "Manual" mode and cook for 2 minutes at High pressure. Oncecooking is complete, use a quick pressure release; carefully remove the lid.
Serve in a nice bowl, sprinkle the sesame seeds over the top and enjoy

Crispy Chicken Drumettes

(Ready in about 30 minutes | Servings 6)

Per serving: 212 Calories; 10.7g Fat; 4.6g Carbs; 23.6g Protein; 3.2g Sugars

Ingredients

1 ½ pounds chicken drumettes
Kosher salt, to taste
1/2 teaspoon mixed peppercorns, crushed
1/2 teaspoon cayenne pepper
1 teaspoon shallot powder
1 teaspoon garlic powder
1/2 stick butter, melted
2 tablespoons hot sauce
1 tablespoon fish sauce
1/3 cup ketchup

Directions

Prepare your Instant Pot by adding 1 cup of water and metal trivet to its bottom. Place thechicken drumettes on the trivet.
Secure the lid. Choose the "Manual" mode and High pressure; cook for 6 minutes. Once cookingis complete, use a natural pressure release; carefully remove the lid.
Toss the chicken wings with the remaining ingredients.
Arrange the chicken wings, top side down, on a broiler pan. Place rack on top. Broil for 10minutes; flip over and broil for 10 minutes more.
Top with the remaining sauce and serve immediately.

Party Deviled Eggs

(Ready in about 20 minutes | Servings 8)

Per serving: 138 Calories; 10.4g Fat; 1.2g Carbs; 9.1g Protein; 0.7g Sugars

Ingredients
1 ½ cups water
8 eggs
3 teaspoons mayonnaise
1 tablespoon sour cream
1 teaspoon gourmet mustard
1/2 teaspoon hot sauce
1/3 teaspoon ground black pepper
Crunchy sea salt, to taste
3 tablespoons fresh chives, thinly sliced

Directions
Pour the water into the base of your Instant Pot.

Now, arrange the eggs in the steaming basket. Transfer the steaming basket to the Instant Pot.

Secure the lid and choose the "Manual" function; cook for 13 minutes at Low pressure. Oncecooking is complete, use a quick release; remove the lid carefully.

Peel the eggs under running water. Remove the yolks and smash them with a fork; reserve.

Now, mix the mayonnaise, sour cream, gourmet mustard, hot sauce, black pepper, and salt; addreserved yolks and mash everything.

Fill the whites with this mixture, heaping it lightly. Garnish with fresh chives and place in therefrigerator until ready to serve. Bon appétit!

Desserts

Cherry and Almond Crisp Pie

(Ready in about 15 minutes | Servings 4)

Per serving: 335 Calories; 13.4g Fat; 60.5g Carbs; 5.9g Protein; 38.1g Sugars

Ingredients
1 pound sweet cherries, pitted
1 teaspoon ground cinnamon
1/3 teaspoon ground cardamom
1 teaspoon pure vanilla extract
1/3 cup water
1/3 cup honey
1/2 stick butter, at room temperature
1 cup rolled oats
2 tablespoons all-purpose flour
1/4 cup almonds, slivered
A pinch of salt
A pinch of grated nutmeg

Directions
Arrange the cherries on the bottom of the Instant Pot. Sprinkle cinnamon, cardamom, and vanillaover the top. Add water and honey.
In a separate mixing bowl, thoroughly combine the butter, oats, and flour. Spread toppingmixture evenly over cherry mixture.
Secure the lid. Choose the "Manual" mode and High pressure; cook for 10 minutes. Oncecooking is complete, use a natural pressure release; carefully remove the lid.
Serve at room temperature. Bon appétit!

Country-Style Apples
(Ready in about 10 minutes | Servings 4)

Per serving: 128 Calories; 0.3g Fat; 34.3g Carbs; 0.5g Protein; 27.5g Sugars

Ingredients
4 apples
1 teaspoon ground cinnamon
1/2 teaspoon ground cloves
2 tablespoons honey

Directions
Add all ingredients to the inner pot. Now, pour in 1/3 cup of water. Secure the lid. Choose the "Manual" mode and cook for 2 minutes at High pressure. Oncecooking is complete, use a quick pressure release; carefully remove the lid.
Serve in individual bowls. Bon appétit!

Cranberry-Maple Rice Pudding

(Ready in about 20 minutes | Servings 4)

Per serving: 403 Calories; 6.6g Fat; 75.6g Carbs; 9.8g Protein; 31.9g Sugars

Ingredients
1 cup white rice
1 ½ cups water
A pinch of salt
2 cups milk
1/3 cup maple syrup
2 eggs, beaten
1 teaspoon vanilla extract
1/4 teaspoon cardamom
A pinch of grated nutmeg
1/2 cup dried cranberries

Directions
Place the rice, water, and salt in the inner pot of your Instant Pot. Secure the lid. Choose the "Manual" mode and cook for 3 minutes at High pressure. Once cooking is complete, use a natural pressure release for 10 minutes; carefully remove the lid.

Add in the milk, maple syrup, eggs, vanilla extract, cardamom, and nutmeg; stir to combine well.

Press the "Sauté" button and cook, stirring frequently, until your pudding starts to boil. Press the "Cancel' button. Stir in the dried cranberries.

Pudding will thicken as it cools. Bon appétit!

Perfect Holiday Cupcakes

(Ready in about 40 minutes | Servings 4)

Per serving: 497 Calories; 17.8g Fat; 77g Carbs; 9.8g Protein; 48.5g Sugars

Ingredients

1 cup cake flour
1 ½ teaspoons baking powder
A pinch of salt
1/4 teaspoon ground cardamom
1/4 teaspoon ground cinnamon
1 teaspoon vanilla extract
1 egg
1/2 cup honey
1/4 almond milk
4 ounces cream cheese
1/3 cup powdered sugar
1 cup heavy cream, cold

Directions

In a mixing bowl, thoroughly combine the flour, baking powder, salt, cardamom, cinnamon, andvanilla.

Then, gradually add in the egg, honey, and milk. Mix to combine well.

Now, spoon the batterinto silicone cupcake liners and cover them with foil.

Place 1 cup of water and a metal trivet in your Instant Pot. Lower your cupcakes onto the trivet.

Secure the lid. Choose the "Manual" mode and cook for 25 minutes at High pressure. Oncecooking is complete, use a natural pressure release for 10 minutes; carefully remove the lid.

While the cupcakes are cooking, prepare the frosting by mixing the remaining ingredients. Frostyour cupcakes and enjoy!

CPSIA information can be obtained
at www.ICGtesting.com
Printed in the USA
BVHW090759030621
608729BV00002B/535